Retro Australia

COLOURING BOOK

NEW HOLLAND

Retro Australia Colouring Book

Discover your inner artist as you create a world of colour throughout these stunning Australian Retro Illustrations.

Australia in the 1950s through to the 1970s with iconic landmarks from the Sydney Harbour Bridge to The Salamanca Market in Tasmania. This Retro Australian colouring in book covers all states in Australia including the Northern Territory and Queensland.

A creative journey around Australia and a look back at a simpler time of how we use to live.

Cities, lined streets of buildings, classic cars of their time, women in dresses and high heels and men with tailored suits and hats are all on display to fill in the colour of those busy streets and fashion of the Retro years.

This book not only celebrates Australia's past, capturing the conservative era of the 1950s and the vibrant, transformative sixties but also delves into the ground-breaking seventies when disco captured the world.

Transform these pages to bring your flair to each page discovering the history of this remarkable country.

Sydney Harbour Bridge.

Rundle Street, Adelaide, South Australia in the 1950s.

Brisbane Street Launceston, Tasmania in the 1960s.

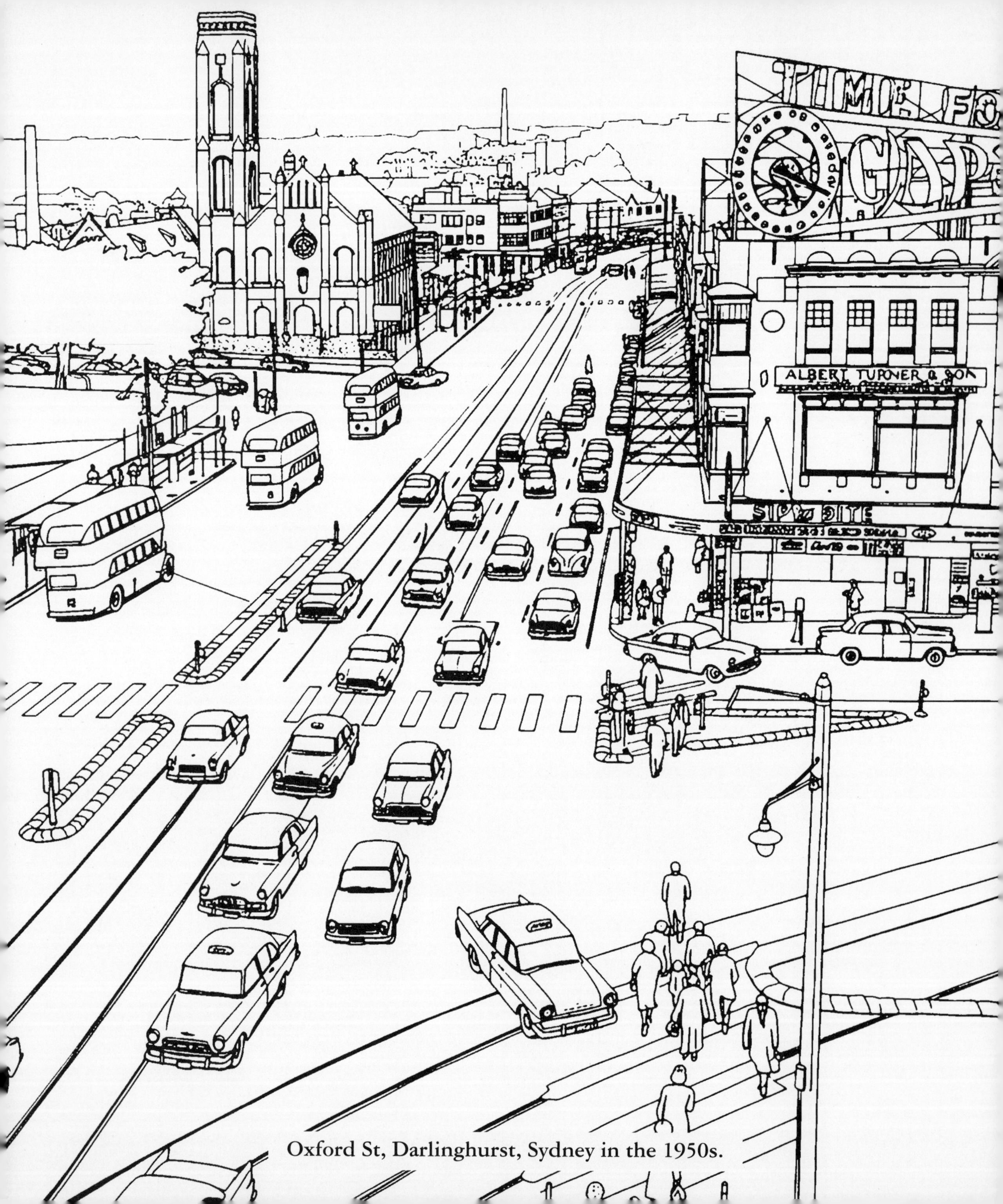

Oxford St, Darlinghurst, Sydney in the 1950s.

Salamanca Market in Hobart, Tasmania in the 1970s.

Melbourne CBD in the 1960s.

M
O.B.M.
PTY. LTD.

Collins Street Hobart, Tasmania in 1964.

Surfers Paradise, Queensland in 1965.

UPSTAIRS

North Sydney in the 1960s.

THE AGE

Elizabeth Street in Melbourne, Victoria in the 1950s.

PARAP GARDEN THEATRE

Cafe in Mitchell Street, Darwin, Northern Territory in the 1960s.

Adelaide Street, Brisbane, Queensland in the 1960s.

ESA BANK

King William Street, Adelaide, South Australia in the 1950s.

COLONIAL MUTUAL LIFE
BUILDING
COLONIAL MUTUAL LIFE
BUILDING

Parliament House, Canberra.

Hay Street, Perth, Western Australia in the 1960s.

The building of the Sydney Opera House in the 1960s.

Alice Springs, Northern Territory in the 1960s.

Kings Cross, Sydney in the 1960s.

Darwin, Northern Territory in 1960.

ACHETTI
BREV

Lygon Street, Melbourne in the 1960s.

Alice Springs, Northern Territory in 1960s.

Plane over Sydney Harbour Bridge.

The Ghan, South Australia to Northern Territory.

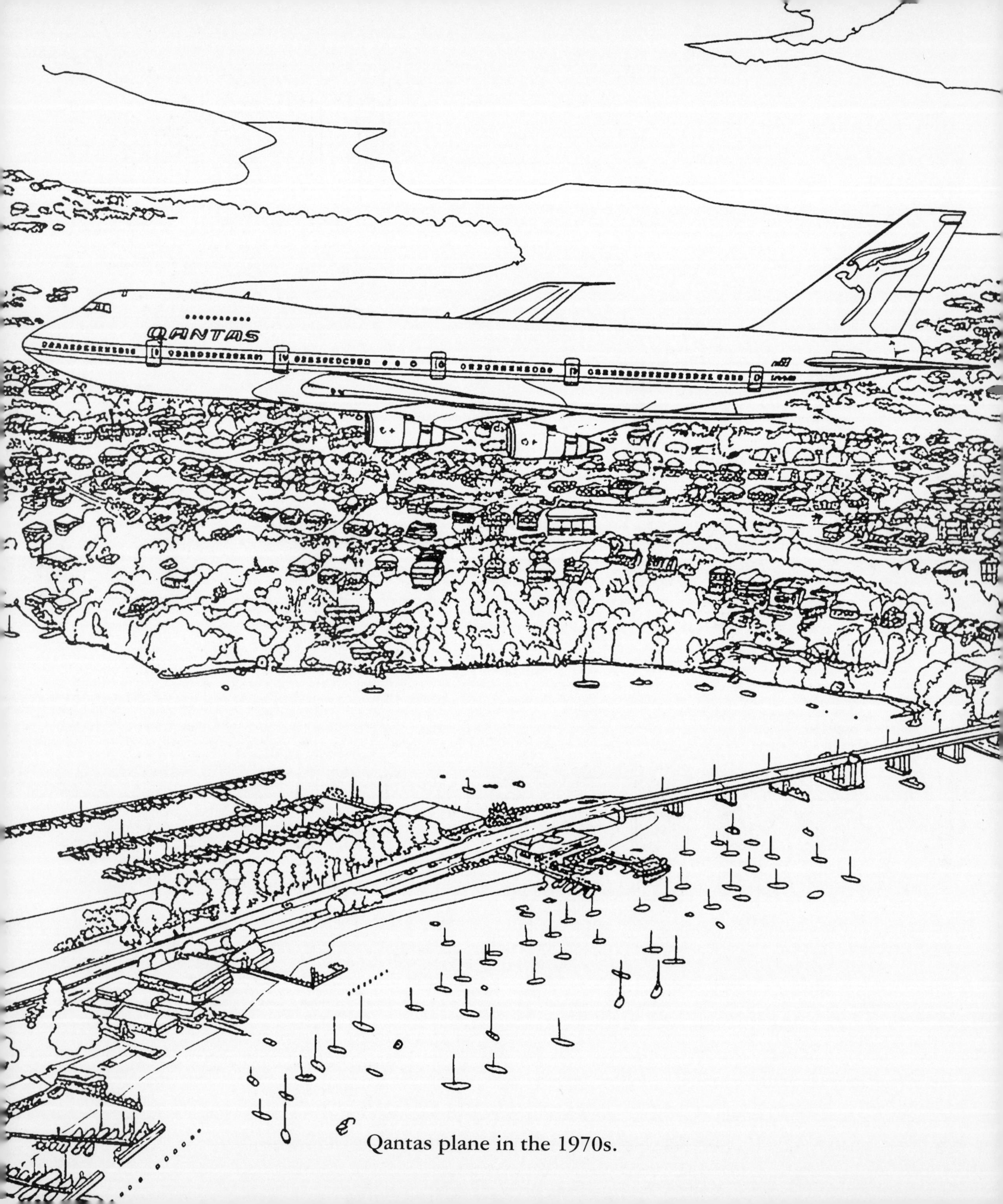

Qantas plane in the 1970s.

Tram in Melbourne, Victoria in the 1970s.

Puffing Billy, Victoria in the 1960s.

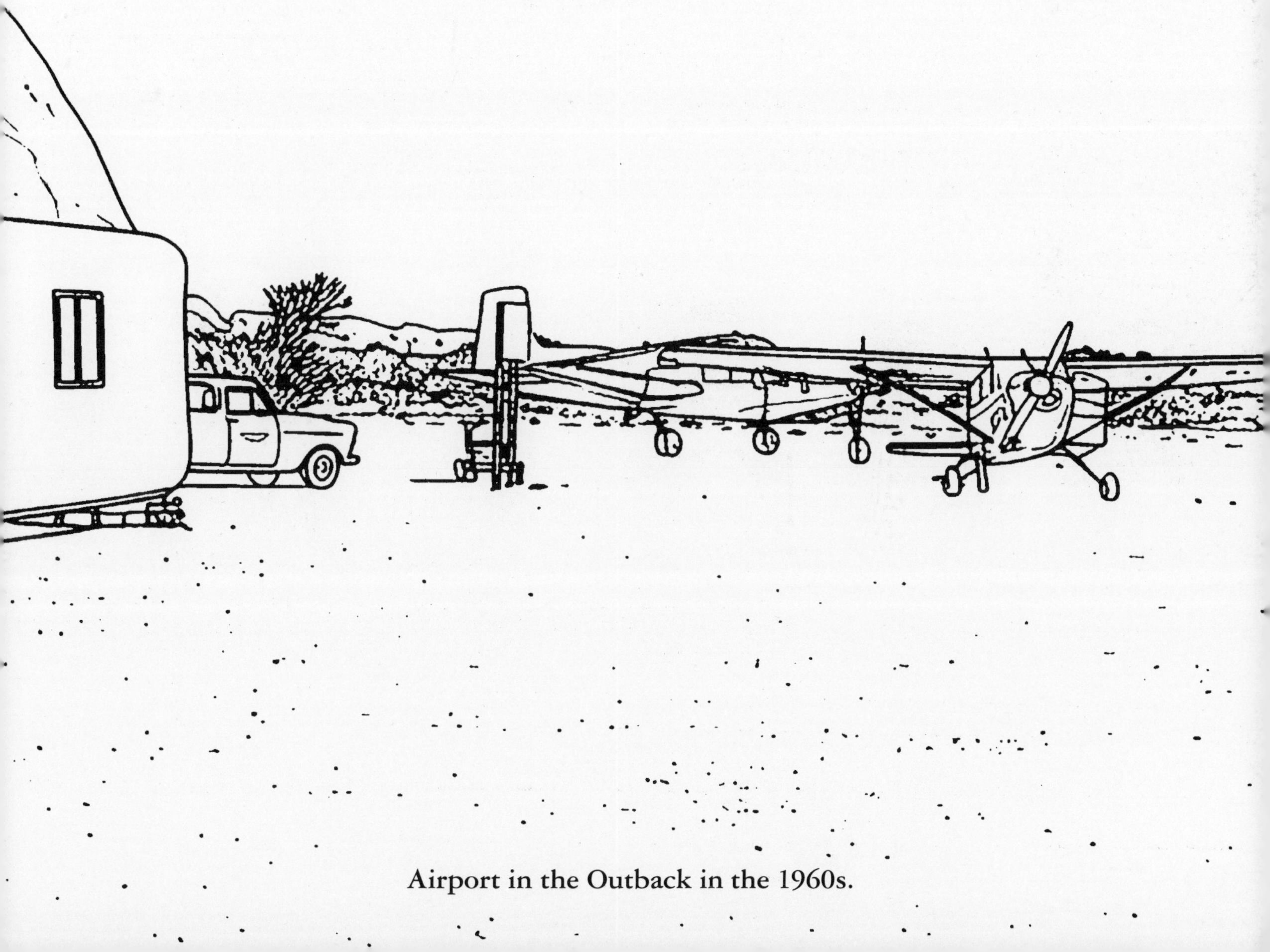

Airport in the Outback in the 1960s.

Service Station in the 1960s.

SHELL
PORT

Family watching television.

Australian House in the 1960s.

Australian backyard with a Hills Hoist Clothesline in the 1950s.

Inner West Sydney Surburb with a row of toilets in the backyard in the 1950s.

Perth Royal Show in the 1960s.

MERRY
GO
ROUND

Alice Springs, Northern Territory in 1967.

ZOOLOGICAL PARK

Taronga Zoo, Sydney.

Brighton Bathing Boxes Melbourne, Victoria in the 1970s.

Seaworld Gold Coast in 1970.

Surfing beach day in the 1960s.

Caloundra Beach Queensland in the 1950s.

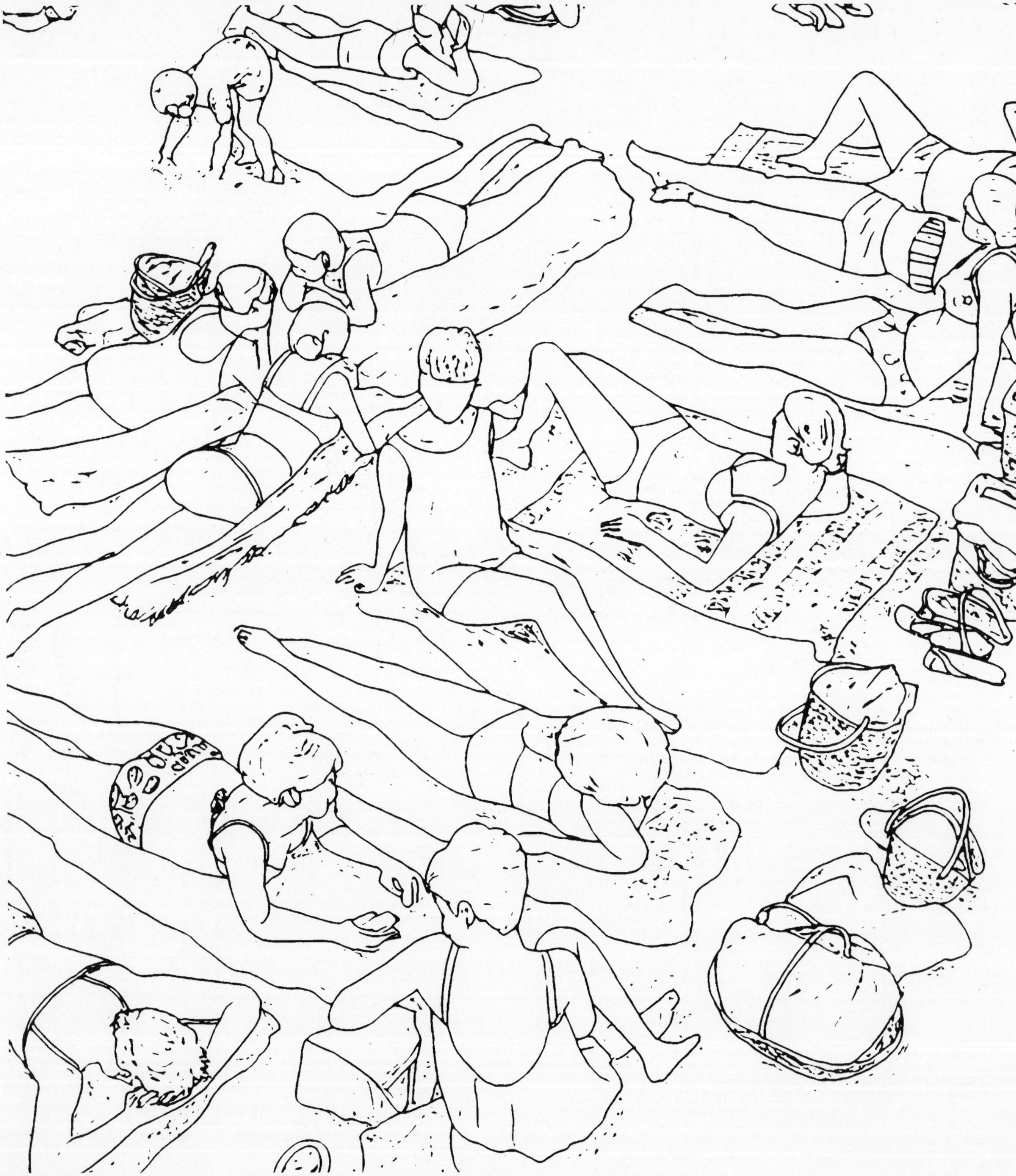

Beach day in the 1960s.

Cottesloe Beach, Western Australia in the 1970s.

Beach at Phillip Bay, Victoria in the 1960s.

Surfers Paradise on the Gold Coast, Queensland in 1968.

Moana Beach, South Australia in the 1960s.

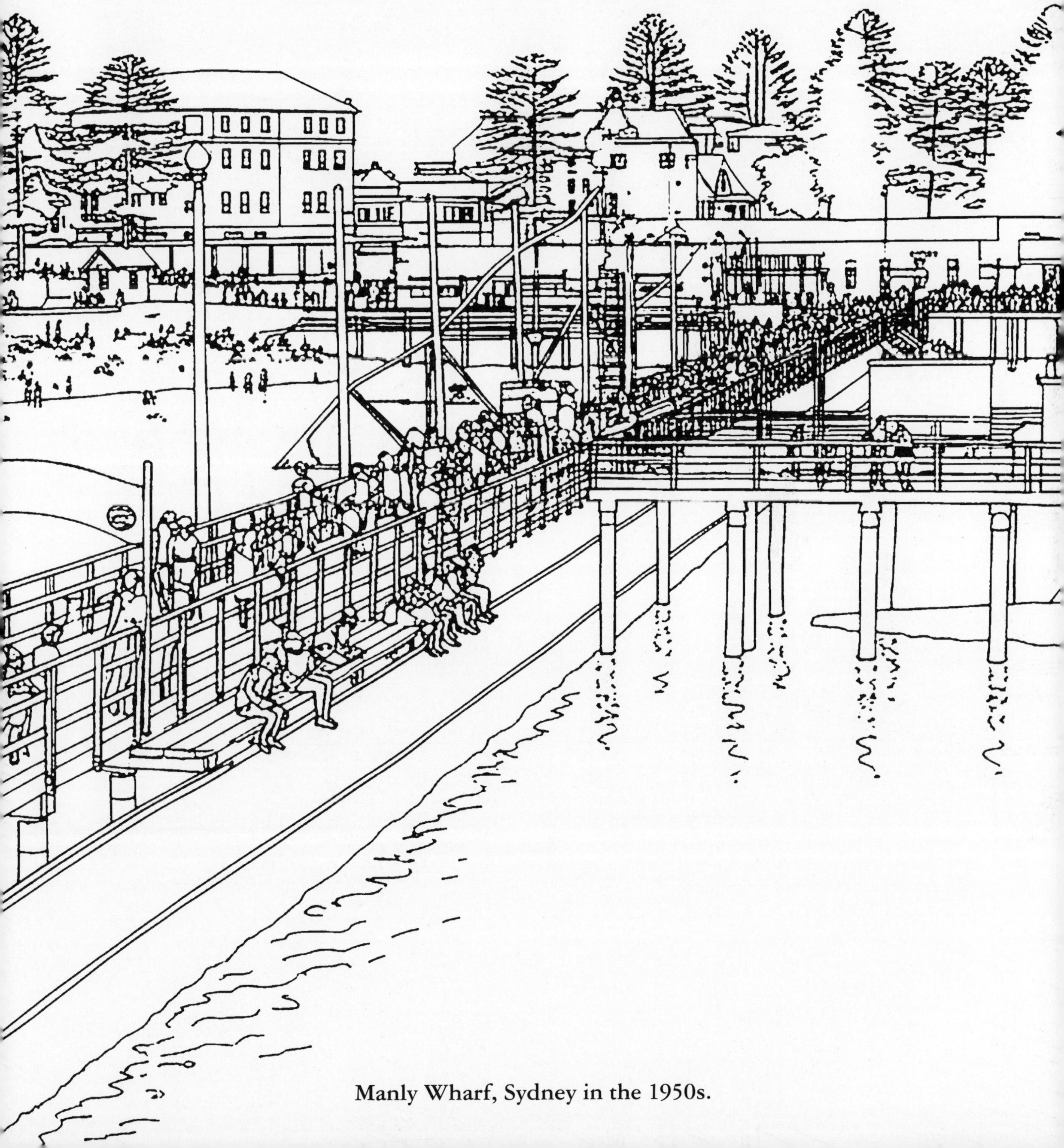

Manly Wharf, Sydney in the 1950s.

NSW Surf Life Saving
Carnival in the 1960s.

Pool Party in the 1950s.

First Published By New Holland Publishers

ISBN: 9781760798659

newhollandpublishers.com

A record of this book is held at the National Library of Australia.